PENGUINS

A PORTRAIT OF THE ANIMAL WORLD

DEREK HASTINGS

NEW LINE BOOKS

Fax: (888) 719-7723
e-mail: info@newlinebooks.com

Printed and bound in China

ISBN 978-1-59764-325-2

Visit us on the web!
www.newlinebooks.com

PHOTO CREDITS
Photographer/Page Number

E.R. Degginger 59

Dembinsky Photo Associates
Barbara Gerlach 15 (bottom), 50, 67 (bottom)
John Gerlach 37 (bottom), 51 (bottom), 66 (bottom)
Eric & David Hoskings 57
Stan Osolinski 66 (top), 69
Rod Planck 5, 36, 39, 49, 60, 61 (bottom)
Ira Rubin 51 (center)
Mark J. Thomas 6, 15 (top), 26, 31, 35, 37 (top), 52–53
Martin Withers 38

Nature Photographers Ltd.
Michael Harris 11

Picture Perfect 28

Tom Stack & Associates
Jack S. Grove 43
Rod Planck 18–19
John Shaw 42, 47, 55, 56
Dave Watts 12 (top), 63

Lynn M. Stone 10, 29

Frank S. Todd 3, 4, 7, 8–9, 12 (bottom), 13, 14, 16 (top & bottom), 17, 20, 21, 22 (top & bottom),
23, 24–25, 27, 30, 32, 33, 34 (top & bottom), 40–41, 44 (top & bottom), 45 (top & bottom),
46 (top & bottom), 48 (top & bottom), 51 (top), 54 (top & bottom), 58, 61 (top), 62 (top & bottom),
64, 65, 68 (top & bottom), 70 (top & bottom)

INTRODUCTION

Emperor and Adelie penguins share the same territories on Antarctica. The Emperor is the largest of all the penguins, standing more than 3 feet (1 meter) tall and weighing up to 90 pounds (41 kilograms). Adelies are much smaller, standing only about 28 inches (70 centimeters) tall and weighing only about 8 or 9 pounds (4 kilograms).

Worldwide, there are more than nine thousand bird species. The penguin family contains only seventeen (or perhaps eighteen) of that multitude, yet penguins are among the best known and most easily recognized of all birds. They are also among the most beloved. The appeal of the penguin is easy to understand. These large, awkward birds waddle along comically with an air of bustling importance. They are extremely tame and curious around humans. And because they walk upright, have flippers instead of wings, and resemble someone wearing formal attire, they remind us irresistibly of ourselves. Not surprisingly, penguins are highly popular zoo exhibits.

Looking at penguins a little more objectively, we find that they remain fascinating for their remarkable adaptations to their hostile environments and for their amazing behavior. Penguins are found in a wider range of climates than any other animal in the world. Emperor, Adelie, chinstrap, and gentoo penguins, for example, all breed on the frozen antarctic continent—the coldest, highest, driest, and windiest place on earth. The Galapagos penguin, on the other hand, is found on the arid and isolated Galapagos Islands, which straddle the equator in the Pacific Ocean far to the west of South America. Several other penguin species are found on the rocky coasts at the tip of South America and Africa, while most penguin species breed on the cold, rugged islands widely scattered across the antarctic and subantarctic regions. When not on land for the breeding season, most penguins live far out at sea in the cold oceanic waters for months at a time. Occasionally hitching a ride on an iceberg, they thrive on the harsh conditions found at the bottom of the world.

Penguin behavior is as unusual as their appearance. These birds have developed noisy, elaborate courtship rituals that take weeks to complete and lead to strong pair bonds that sometimes last a lifetime. Males and females share equally in the strenuous task of incubating their eggs and then rearing their young—a task that takes many weeks.

Penguins are highly adapted to a life at sea. The Emperor penguin, for example, can dive to the astonishing depth of 1,300 feet (over 400 meters) and stay submerged for almost 18 minutes. Scientists continue to puzzle over how penguins can stay underwater for so long without breathing and how they can withstand the changes in water pressure as they dive to such depths and then surface rapidly.

The mystery of penguins is part of their attraction. Although recent research has begun to answer many of our questions about penguins, much about penguin life remains deeply mysterious to us. We still don't know, for example, where many penguin species go when they disperse out to sea after the breeding season is over. We are unable to explain how penguins can gain weight with amazing rapidity and then go without eating, sometimes for weeks on end, as they incubate their eggs or grow a new set of feathers. The answers may help us not only understand and appreciate penguins more, but also understand more about our own bodies.

A group of Adelie penguins hitch a ride on an ice floe—a common sight in subantarctic and Antarctic waters. Sometimes so many penguins crowd onto the ice that others are forced to jump off.

Penguin courtships are highly ritualized and complex. Here male and female Emperor penguins touch bills as part of a noisy ritual that includes loud calling and a wide range of stylized behavior.

THE WORLD OF THE PENGUINS

Penguins are large, flightless, oceanic birds found only on the cold seas of the southern hemisphere. They have flat flippers instead of wings and spend most of their time in the water, diving for fish, squid, and other foods. Because they have very short legs set far back on their body, penguins stand upright while on land and waddle when they walk. Penguins are covered with waterproof feathers that are very stiff and short and overlap tightly above a thick layer of down. Under their skin they have a thick layer of insulating blubber, or fat. The feathers and blubber combine to give a penguin's body a sleek torpedo shape.

Penguins are so distinctly different from all other birds—even other flightless birds such as the ostrich—that scientists classify them in their own separate order, the Sphenisciformes. To emphasize the distinctiveness of penguins, there is only one family, known as the Spheniscidae, within the order. The order and family names come from the Greek word meaning "wedgelike."

This probably refers to the wedge shape of the flippers, although it may also refer more generally to the streamlined body shape of penguins. Within the overall penguin family there are six genera, or groups of similar penguins, containing a total of seventeen (some scientists believe there are eighteen) different kinds, or species.

The six penguin genera are fairly distinctive. The *Aptenodytes* genus (the singular of genera) contains the two largest penguins: the king penguin and the Emperor penguin. The *Pygoscelis* genus has three species—those with long, stiff tails that drag on the ground. The best-known member of the stiff-tailed genus is the Adelie penguin. The two other species are the chinstrap penguin and the gentoo penguin. All six members of the *Eudytpes* genus have unusual crests of colorful yellow or orange feathers on their heads. The rockhopper penguin is one of the best-known members of the crested penguin genus. The other species of this group are the Fiordland penguin, Snares penguin, erect-crested penguin, macaroni penguin, and royal penguin. The genus *Megadyptes* is so unusual that it contains only one species: the yellow-eyed penguin, found mostly on the southeast coast of New Zealand's South Island. The smallest penguin is the "little" or "blue" penguin. It, too, is the only member of its genus, *Eudyptula*. The four

Following page: Adelie penguins are found all over the Antarctic region, including the continent itself, the pack ice, and the scattered islands nearby. They are superbly well adapted to cold weather and seem completely unconcerned with blizzards.

All penguins have short, stocky legs and walk upright. They spend most of their lives far out at sea, coming ashore only to breed and to molt (shed) their feathers. These king penguin pairs stand on typical habitat: a rocky beach on South Georgia Island near Antarctica.

Adelie penguins are starkly black and white. Their heads are ornamented only with eye rings, and even they are simply white against black. Adelies nest in very large colonies on rocky, ice-free beaches.

warm-weather penguins all belong to the genus *Spheniscus.* This group includes the Magellanic, African, Humboldt, and Galapagos penguins.

Penguins are big birds. The Emperor penguin is the largest, standing anywhere from 40 to 52 inches high, with flippers that are 12 to 16 inches long. This robust bird weighs anywhere from sixty-five to eighty-five pounds. A medium-sized penguin such as the Adelie is noticeably smaller, standing about 28 inches (70 centimeters) high and weighing about 8 to 9 pounds (4 kilograms). The little penguin is the smallest member of the order, reaching roughly the size of a mallard duck. The little penguin stands only about 16 to 17 inches (40 to 45 centimeters) high and weighs only about 2 pounds (about 1 kilogram).

From the neck down, all penguins are quite similar in appearance: white on the front, dark on the back. This coloring functions as a form of camouflage when the birds are floating on top of the water. Predators from below, such as leopard seals, have difficulty distinguishing the white underparts of a penguin from the light striking the surface of the water. Predators on the surface have difficulty seeing the penguins against the dark water. The dark feathers also help the penguin absorb the warmth of the sunlight on their backs as they float.

Although penguins stand upright on land, they float on their abdomens in the water with their heads raised, much like other water birds, such as ducks and geese. Because penguins have thick, heavy bones, they float low in the water, with much of their lower body concealed. The importance of the colorful markings on their heads becomes very apparent when penguins are in the water. The colors help the penguins find and identify each other.

All six members of the crested penguin family have thick, heavy bills and crests of long, droopy orange or yellow feathers. The macaroni penguin (shown here) is the largest in the family, standing about 28 inches (71 centimeters) tall and weighing between 11 and 13 pounds (5 to 6 kilograms).

This close-up view of a napping king penguin gives a good look at the unusual feathers. Penguins have very stiff, short feathers that overlap tightly to form a dense, waterproof covering. Underneath is a thick layer of warmth-retaining downy feathers.

Swimming and Diving

Penguins are ungainly on land but amazing-
ly graceful in the water, far more so than any
of the other swimming and diving birds.
Waterfowl, such as geese and ducks, swim on
the surface by paddling with their webbed
feet; diving birds, such as ducks and grebes,
swim underwater by holding their wings
close to their bodies and propelling themselves with their feet. Penguins take a totally
different approach to swimming and diving.
On the surface, they paddle along slowly
by "rowing" with their flippers in shallow
strokes. When swimming and diving, penguins

use their flippers to "fly" through the water
exactly the way other birds use their wings
to fly through the air. They use their feet
primarily to steer, just as flying birds use their
tail feathers.

When penguins want to swim somewhere
fast, they porpoise—that is, they swim just
below the surface, surfacing often to breathe
and travel briefly through the air—rather like
a flying fish—and then dive down again.
More typically, penguins travel by making
short, shallow dives that last for about twenty seconds. They then rest on the surface for
another twenty seconds or so before diving
again. Penguins average between 2 and 4
knots (4 to 8 kilometers) per hour when they
are swimming in shallow dives. They can
put on short bursts of speed of up to 6 knots
(12 kilometers) per hour when porpoising to
pursue prey or evade a predator.

Penguins dive to find the small fish, squid,
and krill (tiny, shrimplike creatures that teem
in the cold waters of the antarctic region)
that are their chief foods. All penguins dive
surprisingly deep and can stay underwater
for a long time, up to minutes on end.
The Emperor penguin can stay below for as
long as 18 minutes and reach a depth of
over 1,300 feet (400 meters). Medium-sized
penguins such as the gentoo routinely dive

deeper than 300 feet (100 meters) and stay underwater for 3 or 4 minutes. Even the little penguin has been known to dive to 230 feet (70 meters) and can stay below for more than a minute.

Very little light penetrates the water at the depths to which penguins normally dive. In addition, there is very little sunlight during the antarctic winter. Even so, penguins manage to find their prey in the dark water. Their large eyes are well adapted for seeing in dim light both underwater and in the air. It's also possible that penguins use their other senses to help find their prey underwater.

Penguins swim long distances from their breeding grounds to reach their feeding areas far out to sea. Most penguins live and breed in the cold ocean region between latitudes fifty and sixty degrees south. A number of cold ocean currents sweep northward from this region. The cold currents meet the warmer waters of the southern Indian, Atlantic, and Pacific oceans anywhere between latitudes forty-eight and sixty-one degrees south. The meeting point forms a band some twenty to thirty miles (thirty to fifty kilometers) wide known as the Antarctic Convergence or the Antarctic Polar Front.

Here the colder, denser antarctic waters sink below the warmer waters of the northern oceans, lifting a rich layer of microscopic plankton to the surface. The plankton are food for krill, squid, and fish—which in turn are food for penguins. To reach the Antarctic Convergence, penguins frequently make foraging trips of hundreds of miles.

The antarctic currents are also important to the warm-weather penguins. Although these birds live in more temperate regions, they still rely on the convergence of cold currents with warmer water to create rich feeding regions. Even the Galapagos penguin, found near the equator, relies on the cold waters of the nearby Humboldt Current, which originates in the Antarctic Ocean, for its food.

When they return to shore after feeding, penguins porpoise as the water gets shallower and then body surf onto the shore or jump out of the water. Predators such as sea lions and leopard seals often lurk in the murky waters near shore, hoping to catch an unwary penguin as it returns. If the penguins see the predator, however, they take evasive action by leaping straight up out of the water in a starburst pattern.

An Adelie penguin flees for its life from an attacking leopard seal. Adelie penguins have a high mortality rate, due to leopard seals and other predators. Most Adelies don't survive for more than three or four years.

This group of Emperor penguins has arrived at their destination by tobogganing—snow is still visible on their flippers.

The distinctive head markings of a king penguin are easily seen in this portrait. King penguins have beautiful orange ear patches and orange or yellow plates made of a horny material on their bills. Males and females look the same.

When penguins run on land, they often extend their flippers backward for balance. To enter the water, Adelie penguins wade right in and then flop down when the water gets deeper.

One good way to move quickly on snow and ice is to toboggan on your belly, as these Emperor penguins are doing. They push themselves along and steer with their flippers.

Penguins on Land

Although penguins seem awkward and clumsy on land, they can actually move quite quickly. Their sturdy legs end in webbed feet; each foot has three toes tipped with strong claws. When they waddle along on land, penguins walk as fast as a human going at a brisk pace—about four miles (six kilometers) per hour. They sometimes run in short bursts with their flippers extended behind them for balance. When going up steep or icy hills, penguins use their strong feet and sometimes also their bills to help them climb. To get up and down drops or across gaps in the terrain, penguins hop or jump with their legs together. Penguins can generally jump the height or length of their own bodies. Before jumping across a crevice in the ice, they lean over and peer across to judge the distance. The champion jumpers are the rockhopper penguins. These tough birds hop along with their feet together when they leave the water and climb up the steep, rocky shores and cliffs of their breeding grounds. When they are heading downhill toward the water, they hop, jump, and even slide, falling often, and then jump in the water feet first.

The southern penguin species sometimes forego walking on ice and snow in favor of tobogganing on their abdomens, using their flippers to push themselves along. Penguins usually walk erect, however. They sometimes cover very long distances on foot. Emperor penguins, for example, may walk over the antarctic ice for more than 120 miles (over 170 kilometers) to reach their nesting sites. Other species nest up to a mile (1.6 kilometers) or more inland from the water's edge.

It's easy to see how rockhopper penguins get their name. These hardy, acrobatic penguins jump, hop, and sometimes fall down steep, rocky cliffs to get to and from their nesting sites on the bluffs above.

Breeding Behavior

Every penguin species has highly individual breeding behaviors. Even so, there are some general aspects that remain the same for all. Penguins breed in large, noisy, smelly colonies—colonies of Adelie penguins may contain half a million birds. The parent birds form long-lasting bonds that may endure for years. To attract mates and reinforce their pair bonds, penguins use a wide variety of ritualized display behaviors and loud vocalizations. To attract a female mate, for example, most male penguins use some form of the ecstatic display. The male usually starts out by beating his flippers slowly and rhythmically while arching his neck and thrusting out his chest. He then stretches his whole body upwards and points his bill at the sky, still beating his flippers. The display is accompanied by a loud braying or trumpeting call. Once a pair has formed, they continuously use different types of display behavior to reinforce their bond during the breeding season. After the chicks have been reared, the breeding pair breaks up and the partners go their separate ways. If they return to the same place the following year at that same time, and if they bred successfully the previous year, the pair will probably bond again. With so many variables to contend with, however, it's not surprising that the "divorce" rate among penguins is fairly high.

To make their simple nests, some penguins make a scoop or hollow in the ground and line it with some coarse grass, pebbles, shells, or sometimes bones. Others raise the nest off the ground by making a pile of similar materials. Since these items are scarce on the treeless, barren nesting grounds, the penguins must jealously protect their own nests while attempting to steal building materials from their neighbors. For that reason, the nests in a penguin colony are generally spaced just

On land, penguins usually live in very large colonies that may numbers tens of thousands of birds. This photo shows just a portion of a chinstrap penguin colony. Chinstraps are the most numerous penguins in the world. Their total population is probably well over twelve million birds.

out of pecking range from each other. A few penguin species, such as the little penguin, make nesting burrows under the ground, while Emperor and king penguins make no nests at all.

Although king and Emperor penguins lay only one egg, female penguins of other species generally lay two eggs a few days apart. During the long incubation period (from thirty to sixty days, depending on the species), the parent birds take turns sitting on the eggs. Because penguins usually have to travel a long distance to reach their feeding grounds, each parent's shift is at least a few days long while the other parent is feeds at sea. The parent left incubating the eggs stays on the nest continually and does not feed. In some species this fasting period is quite long. Male Adelie penguins fast for some thirty-five days, while both male and female macaroni penguins fast for up to forty days.

After the chicks hatch, the parent birds brood them for the next two weeks or so to keep them warm and protect them from large predatory birds such as gulls, petrels, and skuas. The first egg laid is the first to hatch.

By the time the second egg hatches a few days later, the first chick already has an exclusive claim on the parents' attention. Researchers believe that the second chick is insurance against the loss of the first, a strategy often referred to as "heir and a spare." If the first chick survives, the second chick usually dies from neglect, a sad but normal part of penguin life.

Penguin chicks are covered with a thick layer of warm, fluffy down and grow extremely fast. Unlike most other baby birds, they are not completely helpless at birth and do not need to be fed continuously. Once the chicks get larger and don't need to be brooded, they huddle together in crèches while their parents go off for one to three days to feed in the open ocean. When the parent birds return, they find their own offspring among the others in the crèche by calling loudly to it. The young bird recognizes its parent's voice and comes running. Parent birds feed the chicks by regurgitating food into their mouths.

When the breeding cycle is over, penguins return to the open ocean and feed hungrily

Emperor penguins have elaborate courtship behavior. This pair is far along in the ceremony, having reached the point of bowing to each other. Mating will soon take place. The penguin at far left is molting, or shedding its feathers.

When the breeding season is over, penguins return to the sea and feed for several weeks or even months to build up their fat reserves. They then return to land and molt, or shed, their worn-out feathers and grow new ones. Molting takes two to four weeks, during which time the penguins fast.

at sea for several weeks. Once they have built up their reserves, they return to land to molt (shed their old, worn-out feathers) and grow new feathers. While they are molting, penguins can't swim. They must remain on land without eating for the two to four weeks it takes to grow a new set of feathers.

Young penguins are easy prey for large, predatory birds such as skuas. Here a skua, with a wing span of about 5 feet (1.5 meters), makes off with an unguarded young gentoo penguin.

Unattended penguin eggs are an easy meal for predatory birds such as this sheathbill. The nearby chinstrap penguins are lying protectively over their eggs. Eggs and young birds on the edges of the nesting colony are easier targets.

Leopard seals are a major predator on penguins. Here a group of Adelies on the Antarctic pack ice is threatened as a leopard seal hauls itself out of the water. More often, the seals lie in wait just under the surface of the water.

Threats to Penguins

Although parent birds vigorously protect their eggs and young chicks, large predatory birds such as skuas, petrels, gulls, sheathbills, and others sometimes steal eggs and unguarded chicks. They also seize chicks from the fringes of crèches. Eggs and chicks are also sometimes lost to sudden downpours or blizzards. The eggs and young of penguins such as the little penguin, which nests on islands also inhabited by humans, are vulnerable to attack by introduced animals such as dogs, cats, and ferrets. During the molting period, penguins on land are vulnerable to large predatory birds such as skuas and petrels.

At sea, penguins are vulnerable to sea mammals such as leopard seals and orcas. Sea leopards, which can reach 11 feet (3 meters) in length and weigh 900 pounds (410 kilograms), often lurk in the murky waters just offshore from the nest colonies and seize penguins as they enter or leave the water. Other threats to penguins include fur seals, sea lions, and occasionally, sharks.

In the nineteenth century, millions of penguins were slaughtered for their oil, which was used as lamp fuel, as a base for paint, and as an industrial lubricant. A major rendering operation on Macquarie Island slaughtered hundreds of thousands of royal penguins from 1895 to 1920 until the island was declared a sanctuary. Similar operations on other islands, including the Falkland Islands, South Georgia Island, and Heard Island, slaughtered millions more. The demand for penguin oil peaked by 1870, however, and penguins have since recovered their former large numbers.

The extensive whaling industry of the nineteenth century actually benefited penguins by removing their major competitor for food. Today, however, increased fishing for krill, squid, and fin fish in the waters of the subantarctic region is putting pressure on some penguin populations. The biggest threats to penguins today are pollution from oil spills, which is very damaging to penguins on the coasts of Africa and South America, and

Following page: A colony of breeding penguins is a noisy, smelly place. In this colony of king penguins, note how the birds stand evenly spaced just out of pecking range of each other. The large brown birds are juvenile penguins still covered with their downy first feathers.

global warming, which may seriously disrupt the ecology of the antarctic and subantarctic region. A large hole in the atmosphere's ozone layer is located above Antarctica. The increased ultraviolet radiation striking the water may cause a decrease in the amount of krill, which in turn could cause a population crash among species that are higher on the food chain. Global warming has already caused large pieces of the antarctic ice shelf to break off; the larger ecological consequences of global warming remain to be seen.

How Penguins Get Their Name

When early European explorers such as Ferdinand Magellan reached the cold seas and rocky coasts of the southern hemisphere in the early 1500s, they were baffled by the penguins they encountered. These weird creatures swam underwater like fish, had flippers like seals, and had strange feathers unlike any other birds. In their coloration and life at sea, however, the penguins strongly resembled auks, northern hemisphere birds already familiar to Europeans who sailed to the great fishing grounds of the Grand Banks near Greenland. The great auk (now extinct) was about the size of the new creatures and was also flightless, although it, like all the auks, had wings instead of flippers. The explorers eventually decided that these new creatures were birds as well. They probably called them penguins because of their resemblance to the great auk, which was known to the Spanish fishermen as the *penguigo*, from the Latin word *pinguis*, meaning "fat." Another school of thought says that penguins got their name from Welsh sailors, who called them *pen gwyn*, meaning "white head" in Welsh.

As this Emperor penguin shows, penguins have flippers where other birds have wings. On land, they use their flippers for balance, to help them toboggan, and sometimes as weapons in disputes with other penguins.

All penguins have flat, powerful flippers instead of wings, as this king penguin shows. Penguins use their flippers to "fly" through the water, just as other birds fly through the air.

EMPEROR AND KING PENGUINS

Emperor and king penguins are the two members of genus *Aptenodytes* (meaning "unwinged diver"). As its name suggests, the Emperor is the largest of all penguins, often standing more than three feet (over one meter) tall and weighing up to ninety pounds (forty-one kilograms). The king penguin is the second-largest penguin, reaching between 34 to 38 inches (85 to 95 centimeters) in height and weighing anywhere from 26 to 31 pounds (12 to 14 kilograms). Both species have long, thin, slightly downward-curving bills ornamented with orange and pink plates. Their heads are adorned with beautiful golden ear patches. Unlike all other penguins, the Emperor and king penguins use no nests and lay only one, not two, eggs.

Emperor Penguins

Emperor penguins breed exclusively on the continent of Antarctica and rarely venture north of the Antarctic Convergence. King penguins live on antarctic and subantarctic islands such as Macquarie Island and South Georgia Island. They are found on both sides of the Antarctic Convergence, and are sometimes even seen on the Patagonian coast of South America.

Emperor penguins have one of the most unusual and fascinating breeding strategies in the bird world. Courtship begins in March, in the antarctic autumn. Males and females come ashore onto the pack ice that has formed around the coast of the continent. They then walk inland as far as 120 miles (200 kilometers) to reach their inland breeding colonies, trudging forward through steadily worsening weather in long lines. Because they come ashore as the winter approaches, most Emperor penguins never set foot on anything but ice. About thirty-five breeding colonies are scattered around the coast of Antarctica. The colonies are

To climb out of the water onto the pack ice, penguins use the claws on their strong feet, often assisted by their powerful beaks.

Emperor penguins breed in the depths of winter on the frozen Antarctic continent. The chicks are hatched in July, during the Antarctic winter, and are ready to go to sea by themselves by January.

29

extremely large. The Cape Washington colony, for example, ordinarily contains some twenty to twenty-five thousand breeding pairs, while the colonies in the Ross Sea sector contain some eighty thousand breeding pairs.

Once at the breeding sites, Emperor penguins do not seek out earlier mates in order to bond again. The male Emperor advertises for a new mate by standing with his head on his chest and calling loudly. An interested female stands facing him. The two penguins slowly lift their heads and stretch themselves up as tall as they can. The process is repeated several times. A pair bond quickly forms and is reinforced over the next six weeks or so. Emperor penguins do not build a nest of any sort. Instead, the female Emperor penguin lays a single, large egg that is about the size of a softball. The male penguin immediately uses his bill to scoop the egg onto the top of his feet, where it is covered and warmed by a

A young Emperor chick rests on its parent's feet. The parent bird protects the chick against the Antarctic cold by a covering it with a thick fold of abdominal skin. This chick is only a few days old.

Antarctica is the coldest, driest, highest, and windiest place on earth. In the depths of winter there, the sun never shines and temperatures can drop to −140 degrees F (−60 degrees C). In one of nature's most amazing adaptations, Emperor penguins raise their young in this hostile environment during its most difficult season.

fold of skin in the abdomen. The female penguin then leaves, returning across the ice to feed in the distant open sea. For the entire nine-week incubation period, in the depths of the dark antarctic winter, the male Emperor will withstand temperatures that drop to –140 degrees Fahrenheit (–60 degrees Celsius) and winds that reach 300 miles (480 kilometers) per hour, all without eating. The males survive in this incredibly hostile environment by huddling together in dense masses to share their body heat. The huddle is in slow, constant motion as penguins on the colder outside edge gradually work inward toward the center, while those in the center are slowly pushed outward. Between fasting for six weeks during courtship and nine weeks during incubation, male Emperor penguins lose about half their body weight. They very rarely die of starvation, however. If the male's reserves drop too low, he will abandon the egg and return to the sea to feed.

Immediately after she lays her egg, the female Emperor penguin transfers it to her mate. He will incubate the egg by holding it on top of his feet for the next nine weeks, until it hatches. The female heads out to sea to feed and will return only after the egg hatches.

After some seven weeks of brooding by the parent birds, young Emperor penguins form groups, or crèches, and huddle together for protection and warmth while their parents forage at sea. The parents will continue to feed the young bird for several more months.

Even after a young Emperor penguin is too big to be brooded under the parent's abdominal fold, it must still be kept warm. The young bird here stands on its parent's feet. When brooding its young, the adult penguin leans back on its "heels" to keep its own feet from contact with the ice.

When the egg hatches, the male broods (warms and protects) the tiny chick on top of his feet, just as he incubated the egg. The female penguin usually returns within a few days of the hatching. If the female is late or doesn't return, the male, now near the end of his ability to fast, abandons the chick.

The returning female quickly finds her mate and newborn chick and takes over the brooding duties. She also feeds the chick, regurgitating food into its mouth. The male goes off to feed for a few days and then returns to feed the chick and trade places with the female. The pair will continue to trade places until the chick is full grown in December, at the height of the antarctic summer. During this time, long lines of penguins trudge back and forth to the water's edge to provide the rapidly growing chicks with the nourishment they need.

By the time the chicks are about seven weeks old, they are covered with a thick, fluffy down and are too large to be brooded. Instead, the chicks huddle together for warmth and protection in large crèches. The parent birds call to their offspring when they arrive with food. By December, when the young birds are nearly full grown, their parents virtually abandon them. On a warm, sunny day, groups of young birds follow the adults to the water's edge and simply dive in. They seem to know instinctively how to swim, dive, and catch their prey. All the birds, adults and juveniles alike, disperse to sea to feed in the teeming summer waters. They will return to shore in late January and February for a few weeks to molt and grow new feathers. Shortly after that, the breeding cycle will begin again. Emperor penguins don't reach breeding age until they are at least four years old. They usually live for twenty years or longer.

When it's feeding time, parent Emperor penguins call to their young in the crèche. The young bird recognizes its parent's voice and runs up to be fed.

Opening wide, a young Emperor chick waits for a parent to regurgitate food into its mouth. The parents usually take turns feeding the young. When one parent arrives to feed the chick, the other heads out to sea to feed.

King penguins breed on the scattered, rocky islands found in the Antarctic and subantarctic region. Their breeding season is in the summer, when temperatures are milder and food easy to find.

By the time Emperor penguin chicks are a few months old, the Antarctic spring has begun. When the young birds go to sea for the first time in early summer, the days will be almost twenty-four hours long and food in the ocean will be abundant.

King Penguins

King penguins also have an unusual breeding cycle. Male king penguins incubate the egg much as Emperors do, but they do so in far milder summer weather. The female leaves to forage at sea right after laying, but she returns about three weeks later to take over from the male. In all, the male penguin must fast for only a little more than a month. When the chick hatches after fifty-four days, it is fed only about twice a week by each parent, or roughly once every other day. Even so, the chicks grow very fast in the warm summer conditions and put on a thick layer of blubber. When autumn arrives, the adult king penguins disperse out to sea, leaving their

This breeding colony of king penguins is found on the Falkland Islands. The male birds incubate the eggs on top of their feet for about three weeks. The females then return and take over; the eggs hatch nearly five weeks later.

chicks, still covered in fluffy down, to survive the cold season almost entirely on their own. The chicks must rely on their stored fat, although the parent birds may occasionally come ashore and feed them. To keep warm and avoid predators, the chicks huddle together, much as Emperor penguins do. The parent birds arrive back at the breeding colony in the spring and start feeding their hungry offspring again. In another two months, each chick has its adult feathers and is ready to go off on its own. By that point, however, it may be too late into the next

breeding season for the parent birds to raise another chick, so king penguins usually breed successfully only every other year.

Recent research has revealed more about the mysterious life of a king penguin at sea. No matter where they breed, king penguins travel to the Antarctic Convergence region to feed on tiny lanternfish. On a single foraging trip of two to three weeks, a king penguin may cover a distance of more than 900 miles (1,440 kilometers). They dive to depths of between 600 and 900 feet (180 to 270 meters) and stay below for 5 to 7 minutes.

Following page: When a king penguin preens its shoulders and the upper parts of its flippers, it is often indicating uneasiness or aggression.

Looking more like an overstuffed fur muff than a bird, a juvenile king penguin drowses in the sun. The thick layer of brown down helps keep it warm, but even more important for warmth is the thick layer of blubber, or fat, beneath its skin.

King penguins keep their feet dry by standing on gravel bars in the shallow coastal waters of South Georgia Island. This windswept, barren island is home to large breeding colonies of king, gentoo, macaroni, and chinstrap penguins.

STIFF-TAILED PENGUINS

The stiff-tailed penguins—Adelies, gentoos, chinstraps—all have long, bristly tails that sweep the ground behind them and also act as props. Although these birds are similar in size and share some appearance characteristics, their behavior is quite different. During the breeding season, all three species are found on or near the Antarctic Peninsula. During the rest of the year, however, Adelies stay near the pack ice off Antarctica, while the chinstraps migrate north into warmer waters. Gentoos usually stay near their breeding islands.

Adelie Penguins

The Adelie is the most widely distributed penguin in the antarctic region. Because the population is so large and tame, Adelies are probably the most studied of all the penguins. These attractive, short-billed penguins are almost completely unadorned, with the exception of white eye rings that stand out sharply against their black heads. Adelies are smallish penguins that stand only about 28

Adelie penguins are found throughout the Antarctic region. The largest breeding colonies are found along the coastline of the Antarctic continent, with others on the rocky islands in the region.

Although Adelie penguins occasionally venture as far as the coastlines of South America and southern Africa, they are not found in the open ocean very often. Instead, they prefer water filled with floating pieces of ice (pack ice).

Members of the stiff-tailed penguin family, including these Adelie penguins, have long, pointed tails that drag on the ground behind them as they walk.

The characteristic dorsal fin of a killer whale (orca) sticks up menacingly out of the water as it cruises near a group of Adelie penguins. Killer whales often lurk near penguin colonies and pick off unwary birds.

To enter the water, Adelie penguins jump right in, often after hesitating for a long time at the edge of the ice. When many Adelies congregate on an ice floe or cliff, they jostle each other for a while until a few jump (or are pushed) into the water. The first penguin in may be the unlucky one caught by a lurking sea leopard.

Adelie penguins are such strong swimmers that they can literally jump out of the water and up onto the ice, as seen here. Most penguins can easily jump the height of their own body and then some.

"Feeding chases" are common behavior among several penguin species, including Adelies. When the parent bird comes ashore to feed the chick, it runs away, forcing the chick to chase it in order to be fed. The purpose of the chase is not fully understood. In cases where the parents have hatched two chicks, it may allow the stronger chick to survive at the expense of the younger, weaker chick.

Nesting by the tens of thousands on bare, rocky shores, Adelie penguins form huge colonies. The total Adelie population is estimated at over 2.4 million breeding pairs, in addition to unmated juvenile birds.

The only ornamentation on an Adelie penguin is the white ring encircling each eye. This Adelie has been alarmed by something and is in the direct stare posture. Its bill is pointed toward whatever the threat is—perhaps a predatory skua above.

Fresh water is scarce in the frozen Antarctic. Here Adelie penguins take a "drink" by eating snow. In general, penguins don't really need to drink fresh water. Nasal glands at the base of their bills let them excrete salt from the seawater they swallow as they catch their prey.

A pair of proud Adelie parents protect their young chick in its pebble nest. One parent will shortly leave to feed in the open ocean for a few days while the other stays behind to brood the chick.

inches (70 centimeters) high and weigh about 8 to 9 pounds (4 kilograms).

Named after the wife of the French explorer Admiral Dumont d'Urville, who explored Antarctica in late 1830s, Adelies breed all around the coast of Antarctica. Colonies are also found on nearby islands, including Scott Island and the Balleny Islands. In general, Adelie penguins nest on rocky, ice-free beaches in very large colonies that may contain tens of thousands of birds. In total, there are well over 2.5 million breeding pairs of Adelie penguins. Although Adelie penguins show no fear of people, they are very territorial and have no hesitation about attacking a human if they feel threatened. Mated pairs defend their nesting site vigorously with a variety of threat displays that escalate into pecks, chasing, and pummeling with the flippers if

necessary. Pebbles and bones to line the nest are at a premium. The birds are constantly trying to steal them from other nests—and constantly defending their own nests from thievery. Females lay two eggs in a pebble nest and then depart for three weeks of feeding at sea, leaving the male to incubate the eggs both by holding them on top of his feet and lying over them in the nest. As is usual with the heir-and-a-spare strategy, the second chick often does not survive.

Gentoo Penguins

Gentoo penguins have a conspicuous white patch above each eye; the bills are bright orange. Standing 30 to 35 inches (75 to 95 centimeters) tall and weighing about 13 pounds (6 kilograms), they are the largest members of the stiff-tailed genus. Gentoos

In the barren Antarctic region, even pebbles are scarce. Here two gentoo penguins defend their pebble nest from an interloper. Attempted thievery occurs constantly in penguin colonies.

are quite timid and will flee if a human approaches them. They breed on Antarctica and the islands of the subantarctic region, including the Falkland Islands and the Crozet Islands. On the islands, gentoos usually make their nests among the tussocky inland plants. Gentoos lay two eggs. If both chicks survive, they both will try to get the parent birds to feed them. The parent bird runs away, forcing the chicks to chase it to be fed. The larger, older chick wins the race; the second chick is fed later only if food is very abundant. If it is not, the second chick perishes.

Gentoo penguins make a variety of calls and displays during courtship and to express aggression. This male gentoo is calling to attract a mate.

Gentoo penguins are quite gregarious, often forming large breeding colonies. They are found on the subantarctic islands and on the Antarctic continent. Stragglers are sometimes found on the coasts of Argentina, Australia, and New Zealand.

Following page: A small group of chinstrap penguins is dwarfed by the huge iceberg on which they ride. Blue icebergs such as this are very beautiful and very rare.

Many penguins breed on bare, stony ground, but gentoos prefer inland grassy areas whenever possible. They line their nests with grass, moss, shells, sticks, and whatever else is available. Gentoos that nest on Antarctica must make do with pebbles, old feathers, and the occasional bone.

The distinctive white ear patches and orange bill are easily seen on this gentoo penguin. Although these birds are the largest in the stiff-tailed family, they are rather fearful and run away if approached by a human.

Chinstrap Penguins

Chinstrap penguins may be the most numerous in the world; their total population is estimated at anywhere between twelve and thirteen million. These birds are found mostly on the barren islands of the subantarctic region, but a large population breeds on the Antarctic Peninsula alongside colonies of Adelie penguins. At sea, chinstraps are often seen riding on icebergs in groups. Sometimes so many will crowd onto one iceberg that some are forced to jump off.

Chinstrap penguins get their name from a thin band of black feathers that runs from ear to ear under their chins. Chinstraps are just a little smaller than Adelies, standing about 28 to 30 inches (71 to 76 centimeters) tall and weighing about 9 pounds (4 kilograms). They are fairly aggressive birds that have been known to attack humans visiting their colonies. Unusual among penguins, chinstraps raise both chicks.

Chinstrap penguins follow the heir-and-a-spare breeding strategy. The first chick is already a few days old while the second egg has yet to hatch. The second chick is unlikely to survive.

Chinstrap penguins often crowd onto icebergs in large numbers. Here a few chinstraps have decided to dive off again; others are about to follow.

The thin band of dark feathers that stretches from ear to ear under their chins gives chinstrap penguins their name. These medium-sized penguins are widely found throughout the Antarctic and subantarctic region.

CRESTED PENGUINS AND OTHERS

Although Emperor and Adelie penguins may be the most familiar of penguins, the six members of the crested penguin genus are the most colorful. All the crested penguins have bodies with the familiar penguin black-and-white coloration. Their heads, however, are quite vivid and distinctive. All crested penguins have short, heavy, orange-colored bills and red or red brown eyes. They all also have unusual crests of bright yellow or orange plumes sprouting from their foreheads and the area around the eyes.

The breeding behavior of all members of the crested penguin genus puzzles scientists. These penguins generally lay two eggs. The first egg only rarely hatches; the second egg, which is laid a few days later and is markedly larger, is much more likely to hatch. In some cases, the first egg is destroyed by aggressive behavior. Recent research indicates, however, that in many cases the penguins deliberately eject the first egg from the nest soon after the second egg arrives. Why? So far, no one knows.

Rockhopper Penguins

The rockhopper penguin is perhaps the best-known member of the crested penguin genus. It is also the smallest member, standing about 18 to 23 inches (45 to 58 centimeters) tall and weighing between 5 and 8 pounds (2 to 3 kilograms). Bright yellow feathers sprouting from its "eyebrows" form two droopy crests that hang down the side of the head behind the eyes. Rockhoppers are mostly found on the rugged islands of the subantarctic region, but they also range as far north as the southern tips of Africa and South America and the southern coast of New Zealand. About twenty percent of all rockhoppers are found in the colder region south of the Antarctic Convergence. In all, the rockhopper population is estimated at about 3.7 million breeding pairs.

Rockhopper penguins get their name from their behavior and their environment. They

Peering carefully at the rocky road ahead, rockhopper penguins jump along a cliffside trail, moving steadily forward about a foot (30 centimeters) with each hop. On their way up or down they often fall, sometimes for long distances, but always just bounce up and continue on with no apparent damage.

All rockhopper penguins, both male and female, have yellow "eyebrows" a crest of long, drooping yellow feathers sprouting above each ear, and spiky black feathers on the top of the head.

nest in vast colonies on barren, very rugged islands such as Tristan da Cunha Island and Heard Island. Because these island rise almost straight up from the sea, they have no beaches. Instead, jumbled boulders at the shore lead directly to steep cliffs. Rockhopper penguins sometimes site their breeding colonies near the rocky shore, but they generally prefer promontories and steep slopes well above sea level and often more than a mile (1.6 kilometers) inland. The huge colony on New Island in the Falkland Islands contains some three million birds and is located 200 feet (60 meters) above sea level.

To get down to the water, rockhoppers jump with their feet together, slip, slide, bounce, and even fall down the cliffs. They then jump feet first into the water. To reach land from the sea, rockhoppers jump straight out of the water. They jump up the paths that lead to their nesting sites, bounding forward about one foot (thirty centimeters) at a time. These sturdy birds can even withstand large drops onto massive boulders without harm. Residents of the Falkland Islands call them "rockies" or "jumping jacks."

Rockhoppers are very noisy and feisty birds, quick to attack anything, or anyone, that threatens them. In their crowded breeding colonies, the first, smaller egg is often lost to squabbles with other birds from nearby nests. Rockhopper chicks huddle together in *crèches*, but they return to the nest to be fed when their parents call them. Sometimes young rockhoppers have to chase after their parents to get a meal. The chicks grow quickly and are ready to go to sea by the time they are ten weeks old.

To come ashore from foraging, rockhoppers surf in on waves onto the jumbled rocks. They then immediately jump forward out of the water and begin their journey up the cliffs.

Rockhopper penguins breed on the rugged islands of the subantarctic region. Gently sloping beaches are rare here; instead, steep cliffs jut up straight from the water. The rockhoppers make their nests on the tops of the cliffs. To get to and from the ocean, they jump, feet together, up and down well-worn trails along the cliffs.

Macaroni Penguins

The macaroni penguin has bushy orange plumes that meet on the forehead and sweep straight back from the "eyebrows." Standing about 28 inches (71 centimeters) tall and weighing between 11 and 13 pounds (5 to 6 kilograms), it is the largest member of the crested penguin genus. The macaroni likes colder waters and is often found south of the Antarctic Convergence; there is even a breeding colony on the Antarctic Peninsula. The macaroni penguin population is very robust, containing well over eleven million breeding pairs. Macaroni penguins, like rockhoppers, form very dense, noisy, smelly breeding colonies that often contain over 100 thousand birds. The nests are rudimentary, often consisting of nothing but a shallow scrape in the mud or gravel between the rocks on the barren islands. Among macaronis, the first egg is small and very likely to be lost to squabbling; the second egg is larger and has a good chance of hatching.

The name macaroni has the same origin as the line "put a feather in his cap

and called it macaroni" from the song "Yankee Doodle." In both cases, the word refers to the flashy feathers that trend-setting young Englishmen of the eighteenth century wore in their hats. These fashionable fops were said to have introduced the Italian pasta called macaroni to England.

Researchers estimate that there are over 11 million breeding pairs of macaroni penguins. The densely packed macaronis shown here have come ashore for three or four weeks to molt their feathers.

This mated pair of macaroni penguins has made its rudimentary nest of a few pebbles on bare rocks on barren South Georgia Island. Most erect-crested penguins lay two eggs. The first is often broken during nesting squabbles in the dense breeding colonies; the second is the one that usually hatches.

The crest of a macaroni penguin is made of spiky yellow plumes that start as bushy eyebrows and then sweep back behind the eyes. Macaroni penguins are the largest members of the erect-crested penguin family, standing about 28 inches (71 centimeters) tall.

A group of royal penguins wades through a creek on Macquarie Island. These penguins use the creeks on the island as pathways to get to and from their breeding colonies.

Royal Penguins

The royal penguin is found only on barren and isolated Macquarie Island in the Pacific Ocean far to the south of Australia. The island is quite close to the Antarctic Convergence and is also home to king, gentoo, and rockhopper penguins. The royal penguin gets its name from its close association with the king penguins. In size, appearance, and behavior, the royal penguin is almost identical to the macaroni penguin—so much so that until recently, many researchers believed they were actually a subspecies. The only perceptible differences are that royal penguins are slightly larger than macaronis and have more white feathers on the cheeks and throat. Because of these differences and because the two species do not interbreed, the royal is now considered a separate penguin species. Royal penguins breed only in some fifty-seven colonies scattered over Macquarie Island, so they are not as numerous as the other species that breed there. Scientists estimate that there are about 850 thousand breeding pairs.

Fiordland Penguins

Shy and timid, the Fiordland penguin breeds only on the rugged, deeply fissured west and southwest coasts of New Zealand's South Island and on two small offshore islands, Stewart Island and Solander Island. Like the other crested penguins, the Fiordland penguin has a droopy crest of bright yellow plumes extending back behind the eyes. The population of Fiordland penguins is quite small. Researchers can't really be sure how small it is, because this penguin nests in a temperate rain forest environment with dense vegetation that makes it very hard to find and count nests. (It is very easy to use aerial photography to count the nests in large breeding colonies on the barren, vegetation-free nesting sites favored by most penguin species.) By some estimates there are anywhere between five thousand and ten thousand breeding pairs, but other researchers put the number much lower, perhaps as few as one thousand breeding pairs. If the lower number is correct, does that mean the Fiordland penguin is threatened with extinction? As of yet, that question has no answer.

Found in the cool, temperate waters around New Zealand, Fiordland penguins are quite timid. They nest in moist, forested areas near bays and fiords, often building their nests in hollows at the bases of trees.

Most penguins are found widely over a broad area, but the royal penguin makes its home only on Macquarie Island, an isolated speck in the vast Pacific south of Australia. Royal penguins strongly resemble macaroni penguins but are somewhat larger and have more white feathers on their faces. This juvenile has not yet grown its full crest.

Snares Penguins

The Snares Islands chain off the southern tip of New Zealand is the only breeding site for the Snares penguin. This penguin strongly resembles the Fiordland penguin in appearance. The chief difference is the bill, which is much more bulbous in the Snares penguin.

Snares penguins flourish in a moderate climate. The waters off the Snares chain are temperate, and the penguins venture south only as far the subantarctic region. The Snares Islands have a fair amount of vegetation—enough so that Snares penguins are sometimes seen roosting in the branches of low shrubs and trees. The islands of the Snares chain are a marine sanctuary, with no human activity permitted. The population of Snares penguins is protected against interference and seems to be thriving, with some 25 thousand breeding pairs.

Erect-Crested Penguin

A spiky, brushlike yellow crest of long, silky feathers gives the erect-crested penguin a distinctive appearance among similar species. The erect-crested penguin has the curious ability to raise and lower the feathers on its crest—something none of the other crested penguins can do. In other bird species with crests (the familiar backyard cardinal, for example), raising the crest often signifies aggression. That doesn't seem to be the case with the erect-crested penguin. In fact, scientists aren't really sure why this bird raises and lowers its crest.

Erect-crested penguins breed only on four small islands south of New Zealand. the largest colonies are on Antipodes Island and Bounty Island, but small colonies are also found on Oakland Island and Campbell Island. Very sociable birds, they nest in large colonies, often next to or within colonies of rockhopper penguins. The total population of erect-crested penguins is probably around 200 thousand breeding pairs.

Snares penguins breed only on Snares Island off the coast of New Zealand. The climate here is fairly temperate, warm enough to support a fair amount of vegetation and even some trees. Snares penguins follow traditional paths from the rocky beaches up to their nesting sites.

Magellanic penguins are found along the rocky coastlines along the tip of South America and on the Falkland Islands. During the warmer breeding season, these penguins have pinkish bare skin on their faces around their bills. The area is covered with insulating feathers during the rest of the year.

All the penguins in the warm weather family, including the Magellanic penguins coming ashore on the Falkland Islands, have one or two distinct black bands across their white chests.

Warm-Weather Penguins

Penguins are closely associated with the bitterly cold weather of the antarctic region. It's easy to forget that many species prefer a warmer climate. The crested penguins, for example, are basically birds of the cool temperate region of the southern Pacific Ocean. Four penguin species are warm-weather birds that never see snow and don't have to worry about keeping warm. In fact, these penguins have just the opposite problem: They can get too hot. To help them keep cool, they have bare skin, not feathers, around their bills. Warm-weather penguins also make nest burrows to help keep their eggs from overheating. All four species have a continuous dark stripe that outlines their white chest and abdomen. For that reason, the family is sometimes referred to as the "ringed" penguins.

Magellanic Penguin

The largest of the warm-weather penguins, the Magellanic penguin was named in honor of Ferdinand Magellan, who first saw it in 1519 on his pioneering voyage around the tip of South America. This penguin is generally about 27 inches (70 centimeters) tall and weighs about 9 pounds (4 kilograms). It is found on the stormy, rocky southern coasts of South America and on the Falkland Islands. While the birds are onshore for breeding, they are extremely shy and usually hide in their deep nest burrows when humans are around. In the water, however, they show no fear of humans and can be quite aggressive. Although there are probably some one to two million Magellanic penguins and the population seems quite stable, these birds do face some threats. Oil spills are a serious problem. Commercial fishing boats overfish the waters, depleting the food supply; also, the penguins get entangled in the nets.

Breeding Magellanic penguins usually dig deep nest burrows into soft earth or sandy banks; the chicks remain in the burrow for about five weeks before emerging.

The Humboldt penguin has a long, very narrow range. It is found only on the rugged coasts and offshore islands of Peru and Chile. Habitat destruction and other human activities now seriously endanger this penguin.

fertilizer; the resulting habitat destruction caused a serious decline in the Humboldt penguin population, worsened in recent years by commercial overfishing and other human activities. Today the Humboldt penguin is endangered; there are probably fewer than ten thousand birds.

African Penguin

Famous for the incredibly loud and persistent braying noises it makes, the African penguin is often also called the "jackass" penguin. It is found in the coastal waters of southern Africa, rarely venturing more than seven miles (twelve kilometers) from shore. The population of this penguin was sharply reduced in the seventeenth and eighteenth centuries, when the birds were killed for food and oil. Later, guano- collecting destroyed the habitat in many nesting sites. A population that once numbered in the millions was reduced to about 160 thousand by 1993. The African penguin today is a protected species, but oil pollution from tankers continues to be a serious threat. Fortunately, recent conservation efforts have helped these birds establish new breeding colonies, and the outlook is fairly good.

Galapagos Penguin

The most northerly of all the penguins, the Galapagos penguin breeds on the Galapagos Islands straddling the equator in the Pacific. This penguin is the smallest in the warm-weather family, standing only about 21 inches (53 centimeters) high and weighing in at about 5 pounds (2 to 2.5 kilograms). Even though the Galapagos penguin lives on islands where the temperature often exceeds one hundred degrees Fahrenheit (thirty-eight degrees Celsius), it finds its food in the cold waters of the nearby Cromwell Current.

Keeping cool is a big problem for Galapagos penguins. These birds forage in the cold water by day and spend the cooler nights sleeping on land. In the water, they keep their flippers submerged in the cooler water below the surface. On land, they shade their feet with their bodies to keep them cool and hold their wings out at an angle to increase heat loss. In very hot weather, the birds pant, much as dogs do. Birds that aren't incubating eggs or guarding chicks jump into the water to cool off.

Another name for the African penguin is jackass penguin, for the extremely loud braying sounds it makes. The African penguin is also called the black-footed penguin for its unusual large black feet.

Humboldt Penguins

Sometimes called the Peruvian penguin, the Humboldt penguin takes its name from the cold Humboldt Current that flows past the long coastlines of Peru and Chile and supports the rich fishing grounds there. For centuries, these penguins bred undisturbed on the rugged coast and offshore islands. Their droppings, or guano, accumulated in the colonies, sometimes to great depths. This guano was once heavily mined for use as a

The Galapagos Islands are famous for the tameness of their native animals, and the penguins are no exception. In the past, their lack of fear of humans made them easy to hunt down for food and oil. Human settlement of some of the islands has brought new predators such as dogs, cats, and goats, which have reduced the penguin population. Galapagos penguins breed only when the food supply in the cold ocean current is ample. Sometimes, however, world weather events cause the warm El Niño current, which normally flows to the south and west, to move northward and displace the cold waters of the Cromwell Current. This causes a serious shortage of the small fish on which Galapagos penguins feed, which in turn prevents the penguins from breeding and even causes death by starvation. In 1982–83, there was a severe El Niño event that led to a seventy percent decline in the number of breeding birds. The penguins have recovered only slowly from this disaster. Today many researchers believe that the Galapagos penguin is endangered.

Yellow-Eyed Penguins

Third largest after the Emperor and king penguins, the yellow-eyed penguin ranges between 22 to 31 inches (56 to 79 centimeters) tall and weighs anywhere from 10 to 13 pounds (4.5 to 6 kilograms). This bird gets its name from its unusual catlike eyes, which have a deep yellow-orange color. A broad band of yellow feathers extends back from the bill and circles around the eyes and head.

Like the Fiordland penguin, the yellow-eyed penguin breeds and lives on the temperate, forested southern coastline of New Zealand's South Island and on nearby Oakland, Campbell, and Stewart Islands. Unlike other penguin species, yellow-eyed penguins do not breed in densely packed colonies. Instead, the parent birds work

A sea lion frightens off a juvenile Galapagos penguin—this bird is too young to have a chest band. Found on the Galapagos Islands in the Pacific along the equator, these birds are by far the most northerly of all the penguins.

together to build a nest in the forest or dense vegetation out of sight—but not earshot—of other birds. Their nest, unlike the rudimentary nests of other penguins, is a shallow bowl in the ground, carefully lined with grass, twigs, leaves, and other vegetation.

Human activities have severely affected the yellow-eyed penguin. Much of the forest on South Island has been cut down for timber and to convert the land to pasture. The habitat loss has sharply reduced the number of good breeding sites. The birds have adapted by breeding in thick grass, but cows and sheep in the pastures often trample the nests. In addition, introduced predators such as cats, dogs, and ferrets attack eggs and chicks, further reducing breeding success. By some estimates, the breeding population of yellow-eyed penguins on South Island has been reduced by seventy-five percent or more since the 1950s. The populations on the offshore islands are less at risk, but the yellow-eyed penguin is now the rarest penguin and is likely to get rarer. The total population is probably no more than five thousand birds.

Little Penguins

Little penguins are the smallest of all the penguins, standing only 16 to 17 inches (41 to 44 centimeters) tall and weighing only about 2 pounds (1 kilogram). Sometimes called the blue penguin because of its indigo-blue and slate-gray coloring, this little bird doesn't look much like the other penguins. It has no colors or crests on its head and has a stooped over, not erect, posture. Another common name for the little penguin is the "fairy" penguin, a name that seems more like a joke than an accurate description of this aggressive, noisy bird.

Little penguins prefer the relatively warm waters off southern Australia and New Zealand. Because they feed in the shallow, inshore waters, they are fairly common and easy to see from the mainland. They come ashore to sleep every day after dark, and depart again before dawn. The little penguins found on New Zealand have white feathers on both edges of their flippers. Some researchers believe that these white-flippered birds are actually the eighteenth penguin species, but so far most other researchers don't agree.

Little penguins breed in rock crevices or caves; where these are not available, they dig shallow nest burrows in sandy ground. Nesting colonies can be quite large, containing thousands of breeding pairs. The total population on Australia alone is estimated to be at least several hundred thousand birds.

The world's smallest penguin is the little penguin, found in the warm waters off southern Australia and New Zealand. The only penguin to have a slate-gray or bluish color and no other markings, this bird is sometimes called the blue penguin.

Distinctive, cat-like eyes and a yellow band of feathers on the head give the yellow-eyed penguin its name. These unusual penguins are found along the forested southern coastline of New Zealand.

INDEX

Page numbers in **bold-face** type indicate photo captions.